The invisible Woman's Guide to a FABULOUS Future

The 3 Life-changing Secrets for Success

"To plant a garden is to believe in tomorrow"
Audrey Hepburn

Photographic credits

Front cover and spine: Alexas Fotos, Pixabay
Back cover: Aleena Dudderidge

Published in the United Kingdom by Instant Impact Training Ltd
ISBNs (paperback) 978-1-7391818-1-9
           (hardback) 978-1-7391818-0-2
           (ebook) 978-1-7391818-2-6

Typeset by www.ShakspeareEditorial.org
Typographic fonts: Calibri, Palatino
Printed by IngramSparks

Thank you

This book would not have been possible without the support of my own precious sunflowers: Nathalie Mayo my indomitable PA; Sarah Templeton and Rifat Ishaq my witing mates; the fabulous Team Thomson, particularly Peter and Rachel; Philip Radley-Smith visionary extraordinaire; Paul Gardener and Alan Dean for their thoughts; and finally, my clients, who tested this content over many years.

INSTANT IMPACT
Training

The invisible Woman's Guide to a FABULOUS Future

The 3 Life-changing Secrets for Success

Ruth Samuel

We are the music makers,
And we are the dreamers of dreams,
Wandering by lone sea-breakers,
And sitting by desolate streams; —
World-losers and world-forsakers,
On whom the pale moon gleams:
Yet we are the movers and shakers
Of the world for ever, it seems.

"Ode" from Music and Moonlight, Arthur William Edgar O'Shaughnessy

Dedications

This book is dedicated in loving memory of my Mum, Luigia Samuel who taught me so many of the secrets inside it... the hard way! Also, a shout out to my cousin Antonio Ascenzo whose multi award winning artisan Italian ice cream has won decades of prizes, check out La Gelateria di San Valentino in Abruzzo, Citeriore.

Every family has a sprinkling of winners. Encourage yours, become a fabulous role model to inspire your future generations.

Contents

Photo: Alexas Fotos, Pixabay

Foreword

Photo: Aaron Burden, Unsplash

"In seeking happiness for others, you will find it in yourself."

Unknown

"Inspirational and informative. This will change the lives of those who will do the work you suggest"

Peter Thomson

The UK's most prolific information product creator
http://peterthomson.com

A little note from me to you

Legend has it that sunflowers turn their faces towards the sun on bright days and track its course across the sky? But what do they do on cloudy days when there is no sun? They turn and face each other for support. That is what I'm here for, to support you on your dark days.

We both know that women will have a heart-to-heart over a brew and a biscuit to help a friend sort out her problems. Think of this book as a one of those chats. I'll sit with you for as long as it takes. I'll share my best strategies, tips, and experience to help you make your perfect plan, a business plan for your dream life.

I will help you discover your secret weapons that make you stand out. Together we will overcome obstacles and achieve your financial goals. Will it be easy? No, of course not! If it was, everyone would be doing it, but if you create strategic goals with my support, you **will** get the important results you deserve.

By the way, I have used these strategies to help 2,501 people achieve their goals in the past 26 years. I've asked a couple of them to share their personal experiences with you before we set off on your own journey. The first is someone I met over 12 years ago who keeps coming back for advice to this day, the second is a young university graduate who I met more recently. They've done it, they're achieving their dreams and so can you! Here are their messages:

Sarah Templeton, Managing Director, Headstuff ADHD Therapy Ltd

I will never be able to thank you enough for helping me when I was a seriously disgruntled woman but could not see the wood for the trees. I was drowning in a sea of clients and couldn't see a way of carrying on helping people which I desperately wanted to do, without exhausting myself and burning out on a regular basis.

Your ability to see the bigger picture, to come up with alternative ways of doing things and giving me ideas and suggestions literally saved me. With your vision I have now written a bestselling book which is helping more people than I could have dreamed of helping worldwide and my therapy business has expanded from four therapists to ninety in two years. You are exceptional at what you do, anybody reading this book can look forward to having their life changed as much as mine.

Rory Harrison, Graduate Assistant Manager

Having graduated with a 2.1 in psychology, my confidence was at a high, the world was my oyster. However, over the next 8 months doors slammed in my face, interviews went nowhere, I lost my purpose & confidence. In desperation I took a job I hated and with little or no prospects, salary well below my experience.

Through a contact my father had, I was introduced to Ruth Samuel who sat with me and discussed what I wanted and gave me techniques to not only improve my interview skills, CV, and confidence but more importantly the belief in myself. I started to ask myself not am I good enough for this job but is this job good enough me?

In just 3 sessions with Ruth, I landed the dream interview and was offered the role of graduate trainee with a multibillion-pound organisation! Plus, an increase of 40% salary. With a promise of business opportunity and earnings of £100K+ within 2 years. It is my complete belief without Ruth and her work with me, I would never have reached this point. Ruth worked more on my mind than my CV.

Ruth's Top Tip

If you're determined to succeed, you may find it useful to ask someone to hold you to account. I write with 2 good friends, 2 days each week. We support each other, share ideas and experience. You could try working with a family member, friend, or life coach to help hold you to account. Alternatively, email hello@instantimpact.org and join one of my online workshops.

"Nothing is impossible, the word itself says 'I'm possible'"
Audrey Hepburn

Photo: Kata-Kata, Unsplash

Introduction

Photo: Aleena Dudderidge

"Your choices,
Your life,
Your way"

Ruth Samuel

"Difficult roads often lead
to beautiful destinations.
The best is yet to come."

Zig Ziglar

Meet your Fairy Godmother

If you had 3 wishes, what would you wish for? Money? Respect? Validation? If you were guaranteed to win your heart's desire after completing a tough challenge, **would you do it?**

My name is Ruth Samuel, think of me as your real life "fairy godmother". With a pinch of sass and a little bit of feisty, I'll put things right, watch over you and make sure your dreams come true. I will help you get the money, security, and recognition you deserve. I'm a business and educational consultant, mentor, and a qualified teacher. Over 27 years, I have helped 2,501 people get jobs or promotions that they love. I'll use every fibre of my being to match your skills with options that reward your experience.

Your circumstances may change over time so there are 2 **optional** books in this trilogy to offer you additional support:

1. Life-changing Secrets for Success (this book)
2. Strategic CVs (optional)
3. Making a BIG splash (optional)

The 3 Life-changing Secrets of Success

First, we'll take a long hard look at who you are, your personality, values, what you want, what you don't and what your perfect life looks like. Next, we'll draw a treasure map taking you from where you are in life right now to your dream life. Then, we'll action your plan, matching your skills with opportunities. This is **your** personal journey, your sacred *Me Time*, I will travel with you until you achieve the fabulous future you so deserve.

Most people would think the plan is over once you achieve your goals, I'm not most people! The plan isn't over, it just might need tweaking at that stage. Your plan will tell you how long you need to stay in specific stage for, and what additional skills you need to master before taking your next step towards Fabulous.

You are in control of your life, not employers, not other people.

Strategic CVs (optional)

Whether you're going for promotion or new opportunities, you'll need a great CV (resumé). When someone reads your CV, they usually only give you 30 seconds of their time. I used to run a professional CV bureau that offered my clients a guarantee: if they didn't get an interview using their new CV, I'd give them their money back. Obviously, I had to make sure their CVs were powerful, otherwise I'd quickly go out of business! I'll teach you to create strategic CVs and cover letters designed to win **you** interviews in 30 seconds. You'll learn the top 7 mistakes to avoid when putting a CV together... and 3 things you must include to get your CV to the top of the pile.

Making a BIG Splash (optional)

In the third book, well go through interview techniques, create a list of great answers to interview questions from Hell. We will turbo charge your confidence and self-esteem. We'll create briefing documents to take into interviews with you, write templates you can use to accept a job, reject a job, and even use to increase your salary before you start a new job.

By the way, when I say interview techniques, I'm talking about interviews in the widest context including writing press releases, social networking, TV & radio interviews, the whole shebang.

I can help you in several different ways including audio books, social media, podcasts, videos, apps, newsletters, video calls, one-to-one mentoring with me or a member of my team, online training, and spa retreat breaks where we'll work through the activities together. You are not alone. So… take a deep breath, put your big girl pants on and let's crack on.

Who is this book for?

Are you a frustrated woman, at the top of her game … but feeling invisible?

Why is it that the older and more experienced we get, the less confident and secure we often feel? If you are a woman aged 35+, trapped in a "good JOB", where you are **Just Over Broke**, then this book is for you. You have life experience, ideas, and energy but you probably feel invisible and undervalued at work. Ironically, just when you should be the trailblazer that younger colleagues could be watching, your confidence ebbs and you worry about them taking your job.

I'm not being funny but if you're a woman over 35, chances are that you don't just hold down a job, you probably know how to run your home like a well-oiled machine, make the healthcare decisions for your family and manage the household budget. You're probably caring for 3-4 generations including your millennial children, their children and/or pets, your parents and possibly your in-laws as well. On top of all that, you have probably had more education than women at any other time in history and you are more likely to live 10 years longer than your male peers… does that sound inadequate to you? No, of course not! **You are amazing!**

This book brings hope. A combination of your honesty and my experience will create your sanctuary, a special place where you can reinvent yourself away from prying eyes. When you emerge, the world will be dazzled by your shiny new confidence as you enrich humanity with your talents. **Now** is the perfect time to think about the kind of career that would really work for you, one that gives you the financial rewards to afford your perfect lifestyle, that fits in with your values and your commitments.

A note to coaches, counsellors and teachers

Suggesting that someone takes on the tough activities in this book is a big ask. We're talking about completely transforming their life. I have shared some options, and my best proven strategies, but our reader will need **your** support, encouragement, and motivation while they go through this transformation. Most of all, they'll need you to hold them to account while they work through the activities. They are worth our combined efforts. The World needs the unique skills of each one of these women. Bless you for supporting them.

How to use this book

A note to invisible women

Think of this as your journey's logbook, feel free to keep your notes, inspiration, and relevant information in it. You'll learn many new skills along your journey but more importantly this is a conversation between you and me. I'll ask you questions that will make you dig deep; you'll write the answers in these pages and between the two of us we'll create a bank of precious information. You can use this logbook to decide which jobs to go for, write fantastic CVs with, and find brilliant answers for interview questions. Your confidence and self-esteem will increase, **you'll never be the same person again**.

I have left a wide left-hand margin and gaps in the text for you to write your own thoughts. I have also used a different colour for the activities' headings to highlight the tasks you need to complete to create the strategic business plan for your life.

Everyone is different, some of my clients like a lot of space to write in, others prefer to only write a few words. If you need more space for **any** of the activities in this book, please use the jotter pages at the back. You can also use these pages to work up your answers in rough before writing them in the main book. Alternatively, email hello@instantimpact.org and I'll send you a document that expands as you type.

Feel free to customise the pages with stickers, sequins, and ribbons to make this your incredibly special record. The more of yourself you put in, the more life changing this voyage will be.

Photo: "Statue of Labour" by Andrey Pavlov, Shutterstock

Networking

Set yourself up to succeed

Do you remember the sunflowers that I mentioned in my little note at the beginning of this book? How they turn their faces to each other for support on cloudy days? Well, use your own networks in the same way. The beauty of being in your prime is that your friends and contacts have had time to achieve their potential. The little girl you sat next to at school could now be a successful business owner with the skills or contacts you need.

Ask your family, friends, or professional supporters to work through the activities with you. If you make yourself accountable to someone else, you are more likely to stick to it and succeed. It's more fun if you work in small groups of likeminded women, determined to make the best of yourselves.

Roles & responsibilities

I have learned that if you give people first class information, they keep coming back to you even years later. I commit to giving you my very best strategies, secrets and tips that have stood the test of time. In return, I ask you to:

- Say what you think and tell it as it is, be honest
- Be open-minded, try out new ideas and behaviour
- Respect and support yourself, don't put yourself down
- You have experience, please use it
- Remember we all have different opinions and styles
- Involve your friends, family, and other support when you can
- Be jointly responsible with me for achieving your objectives

Outcomes

Put simply, this book is a business plan for your life instead of for a new business. Many of the strategic elements like diagnostics, forecasting and budgeting are rather technical but that's what makes this system so powerful.

By the time you have finished, you will have:

- A personal development plan
- A self-esteem audit
- A skills/qualifications audit
- A personal action plan
- An executive summary (treasure map)
- A strategic business plan
- Personal financial forecasts
- A network of useful contacts
- Sparkly new confidence

Making the effort to build a solid foundation now will give you a great head start when it comes to achieving your potential, writing your CV, and preparing for interviews. You won't believe this now, but by the time you have finished all three books in this trilogy, you will not only look forward to interviews but even feel sorry for the interviewer(s), trust me! ;o)

3

Chapter 1

Right, let's crack on ...

OK, if you're ready, let's dive straight into discovering who you really are. The wide-eyed innocent you once were, the one who knew exactly what she wanted to do or be when she grew up, got swept along by the sands of time. Suddenly you're mature with different skills and priorities. This makes you powerful! The activities in this chapter are designed to work out what's important to you **now**. By the time you have finished them, you will have created a personal development plan; identified 6-7 of your most important values; worked through your self-esteem audit and gained some useful confident communication skills.

Remember, the activities have headings in a different colour to make them easier to spot. Everyone is different, some of my clients like a lot of space to write in, others prefer to only write a few words. If you need more space for any of the activities in this book, please use the jotter pages at the back or email hello@instantimpact.org and I'll send you a document that expands as you type.

I suggest that you put a sticky tab or note at the top of the page you are working on so it's easy to find it later if you take a break. Please take the time to think about the questions and write honest answers rather than race through them and then scamper off to the back of this book looking for answers. The answers will come from you working through the activities and mulling over what you have learned, there are no short-cuts!

Tree of life

TIP: this activity is WAAAAY more fun if you buy yourself a little bag of jelly babies, or other sweets, to munch while you do it! ;o)

Where are you in life?

Where are you on your career path? Look at the cartoon on the next page. It shows a tree with little jelly babies all around it doing a range of activities. Circle the one you identify with today. If you fancy colouring your little jelly baby in, I've put a list of what each colour means at the back of this book (p.74) for a bit of fun.

Why did you pick that one?

Where would you like to be on the tree and why?

You might choose to do this activity at the end of every chapter so you can map your moods. If you do, please write the date next to each figure you chose to make it easier to chart your progress.

Personal Development Plan (PDP)

"The way to get started is to quit talking and begin doing."
Walt Disney

How would you describe your life at this moment?

What do you like about your life at this moment?

What don't you like about your life at this moment?

What do you want to do more of?

What do you want to do less of?

What do you want to keep the same?

What do you want to change?

Your 3 personal goals are:

1

2

3

What do you need to do to achieve these goals?

"When you understand that your self-worth is not determined by your net-worth, then you'll have financial freedom."
Suze Orman

Your most important/urgent goal is?

Your goal is achievable because?

You will know when you are succeeding because you have set the following measurements:

What you need to achieve this
From yourself:

From others:

What information might you need?

What are the obstacles?

Who (person/people) could you ask to help?

Your goal is realistic, you have considered the following risks:

Nail down

Ask yourself on a scale of 1-10, 10 being the highest score:
How strong is my intention to take the first step?

How high is my enthusiasm to take that first step?

How strong is my commitment to taking that first step?

Remember

A goal is only a dream until you TAKE ACTION!!

Break your goal down into mini goals then fill in the chart below to help you keep track of your progress.

Your goal	Action	Start date	End date	How will you know when you have achieved this goal?

Photo: Shedrack Salami, Unsplash

"Fortune favours the brave"
Latin proverb

Disney's Creativity Strategy

If you or I were to apply to our local bank for a business start-up loan to create colourful cartoon films, we'd probably get very short shrift from the Manager! Just imagine how much harder it would have been for Walt Disney to sell the concept for the first time. Mr Disney had 2 weapons: deep self-belief and his Creativity Strategy.

Years later, a now successful Walter Disney built his head office around his Creativity Strategy. The **dreamers** worked on the top floor. This was where the ideas people, creative writers, cartoonists, wardrobe department and musicians worked with their "heads in the clouds".

The **realists**, the people who made things happen including editors, directors, film technicians etc were all based on the ground floor, their "feet firmly on the ground".

The **critics** or accountants worked in the basement. Nobody wanted to go down to the dark and creepy basement, so the accountants were mostly left alone!

When a new script came in, Mr Disney and his associates would run it past the **dreamers** to see what they made of it. With those thoughts fresh in their minds, the team would take it to the ground floor to see what the **realists** made of it. Any technical or practical issues that the realists couldn't solve were taken back to the dreamers to create new solutions. Once the script was considered workable, it was taken down to the basement for the **critics** (accountants) to look at, squabble over and invariably scale back. Any issues that they raised were taken back to the dreamers and/or realists to solve, usually on a tighter budget. If a script survived this process, the film was made and usually became a great financial success.

"If you can visualize it, if you can dream it, there's some way to do it."
Walt Disney

Photo: Everett Collection Inc, Alamy

Stress-test your plan

Walt Disney's Creativity Strategy

You can use Walt Disney's Creativity Strategy to stress-test your personal action plan. Walt realised that you need to co-ordinate 3 sub processes to develop the solution:

- **The Dreamer**
- **The Realist**
- **The Critic**

There would be no ideas without a **dreamer**. However, a dreamer cannot turn ideas into action without the **realist**. The plan might fail if there isn't a critic to ask the awkward "What if?" questions. A critic and a dreamer would just get stuck in conflict without a realist to develop solutions and make things happen.

To do this activity you will need:

- 3 blank pieces of paper, A4 or larger
- Thick felt tip pen(s)
- An obliging friend or colleague
- An open mind

1. Use the thick felt tip pen(s) to draw one large letter on each piece of paper: a D, R or C.
2. Place the 3 pieces of paper on the floor a short distance away from each other.
3. Take up your starting position by standing on the D for dreamer piece of paper. Explain your dream or idea to your friend or colleague.
4. Your stress tester needs to ask you questions that challenge your idea. If their question is about practicalities, they should ask you to move to the R for Realist bit of paper before you answer their question. If they ask an awkward "what if?" question, they need to ask you to stand on the C or Critic bit of paper to answer.
5. Keep moving between the pieces of paper until your stress tester has no more questions left. How do you feel about your idea now? Have you made some adjustments due to the questions? Have you identified some fatal flaws? Can they be fixed?
6. Go back to the D piece of paper. Agree the outcome with the stress tester. Did your idea survive the process? Can you go ahead with it? If yes, take a BIG step forward with a beaming smile. If no, can anything be salvaged perhaps with adjustments? What changes should you make?
7. If there is no hope for your idea then I'm afraid it's back to the drawing board but at least you have saved yourself time, money, and heartache.

Values

Personal or core values

What's important to you in life, I mean very important? Perhaps it's your identity, family, love, health, wealth, or happiness? Values are principles, standards, beliefs, or qualities that are important to you. They are things like career success; security; faith; hope; charity and environment. Values help you live your life your way and make decisions.

Values

Help you make choices
Help you screen and filter naturally
Increase your feeling of direction
Increase your feeling of happiness and fulfilment
Measure the meaning that life holds for you

Life becomes easier when you are in line with your values

The relationship between values and goals

Once you know what your personal values are, you can make clear, rational, responsible, and consistent decisions. Values can boost your motivation and help you to achieve better goals. But if you find yourself in a situation that clashes with your core values, like working in the wrong job for instance, it can cause stress and life becomes more of a struggle.

How values and vision affect your goals

You can combine your values with visualisation techniques to 'live' (try out) your goal for a moment. This will help you to get a feel for the advantages and disadvantages of your goal from the perspective of your values, which will help you plan how to get there more effectively.

Values elucidation

How to fill in the values elucidation table

1. Start by asking yourself "what's **very** important to me in life?" continue asking the question "what else is very important to me in life" until you have 6-7 core values.
2. Although we might share some of the same core values, a word might mean different things to you than it would to me. Take 'love' for instance, you might love your partner and family whilst I adore my cat :o)
   Use the interpretation column to put any explanatory notes e.g., freedom might mean financial security or escaping from an unpleasant situation.

3. Once you have a list of core values, compare each value by asking is "x" (core value) more important to me than "y" (core value)?" For example, is love more important to me than health? Put a stroke (I) in the score box for each value that is more important. Using the above example, if love is more important to you than health, put a "I" in the score box for love but nothing in the box for health. Then compare love with the next value on your list and ask yourself if love is more important than that.

4. Add up all the scores and write the total for each one in the score column.

5. Rank each core value according to how many points it scores and place the final scores in the hierarchy column. 1 is the highest score ranking. Give the value with the most points a top score of 1.

Values elucidation table

Core Value	Score	Interpretation	Hierarchy

List your core values in the order that you ranked them in the values hierarchy column above:

1

2

3

4

5

6

7

How do your core values affect your attitude to work and the world?

What kind of job would suit someone with your values?

How do values affect attitude in the workplace and your world?

Photo: Zoltan Tasi, Unsplash

Self-esteem

So, what exactly is self-esteem?

Self-esteem is a sense of value and worth that comes from a positive self-image. It starts with you and is visible in everything you do. It is the belief that your best is always good enough. Nobody but you can destroy your self-esteem. You destroy your esteem when you do not keep your word, when you do not honour the agreements or commitments that you make. If you say "yes" when you really mean "no". When you don't follow your instinct. You build or destroy your self-esteem in your mind.

People with high self-esteem are usually...	People with low self-esteem may...
Confident, positive	Lack confidence, are negative
Feel in control	Feel out of control
Are optimistic	Are pessimistic
Display assertive behaviour	Don't believe in themselves
Have self-respect	Have little self-respect
Have vitality	Have very low energy
Are comfortable with themselves and other people	Feel they don't belong
Are dynamic	Feel uptight
Make things happen	Say that they can't change
Take risks	Have a victim mentality
Are successful	Feel like a failure
Are charismatic	Feel unworthy
Feel valuable	Don't feel valued
Are decisive	Are indecisive
Feel secure	Feel insecure

Self-esteem audit

Your self-esteem

Answer the following 10 questions and give each one a score out of 10 where 10 = you totally agree with the statement
1 = you completely disagree with the statement

Question	Score
1 My life experience has taught me to value and appreciate myself.	
2 I have a good opinion of myself.	
3 I treat myself well and look after myself properly.	
4 I like myself	
5 I give as much weight to my qualities, skills, assets, and strengths as I do to my weaknesses and flaws.	

15

"Happiness is not in the mere possession of money; lies in the joy of achievement, in the thrill of creative effort."

Franklin D. Roosevelt

6   I feel good about myself.
7   I feel I am entitled to other people's attention and time.
8   I believe I am entitled to success and good things in life.
9   I expect no more of myself than I do from other people.
10 I am kind and encouraging towards myself rather than self-critical.

Add up your total score

The importance of self-esteem

Questions to ask yourself

You gave this a low score – why is this?

What would you like to be different?

What do you praise yourself for?

What do you criticise yourself for?

How would your life change if you were less self-critical?

What 6 things could you do to be kinder to yourself?

Which one is the easiest to do/will bring the greatest results?

What would be the benefits of you doing this?

What needs to happen for you to follow through with this?

When are you going to start?

Once you have answered these questions, write a short reflective paragraph, then read it out loud to make an audio recording.

"Just when the caterpillar thought the world was ending, she turned into a butterfly."
Anonymous proverb

Photo: Devon O'Day, Pixabay

What is confidence?

Thinking with Confidence

Things that happen inside your head impact on your confidence. They affect:

How you think and feel
How you play roles
Your personality
Your ambition
Your ability to get in touch with your 'real' self

Speaking with Confidence

Confidence affects the way you communicate:

How you talk
Assertiveness
Building relationships
Influencing others
Dealing with conflict
Controlling the effects of stress

Projecting Confidence

You can use confidence to impress others by:

Appearing confident
Appearing 'professional' at work
Spreading confidence to inspire and encourage others

Assertiveness

Assertiveness is an important interpersonal skill. Assertive behaviour can often be confused with aggressive behaviour so when you think about developing assertive skills you might worry about being seen as aggressive. It would probably be useful for me to define what these behaviours mean. I'll start with aggressive and passive behaviours because these are the ones that you and I seem to experience daily and then go on to clarify what assertive behaviour is.

Quick Quiz

Before I start, could you please write down what you think **aggressive**, **passive**, and **assertive** behaviour are? Please don't Google them or look them up, just give me your own thoughts.

If you need more space for this quiz, please email hello@instantimpact.org for a document that expands.

Being aggressive means...

Being passive means...

Being assertive means...

"Mother Nature doesn't rule by fear and anger, but by calm strength and assertiveness."

Cesar Millan

Now compare your definitions with my notes below. How similar are our thoughts?

Aggressive behaviour is...

Getting your own way, no matter what
Getting your own point across at other people's expense
Getting people to do things that they don't want to do
Being loud and violent
Interrupting others
Winning at all costs

Passive aggressive behaviour is...

Some aggressive behaviour is indirect, this can include:
Presenting hostility in a polite way
Quiet and apparently inoffensive
Manipulating or tricking people
Ignoring people
Being silent
Using sarcasm
Putting people down, making them feel small
Inoffensive on the surface

Funnily enough, aggressive behaviour doesn't come from being over-confident, quite the opposite, it comes from a lack of confidence and fear. Underneath the blustery bully is a coward. You might find it hard to believe but the person who is having a go at you could be feeling just as threatened as a passive person.

Think about times at home/work when you behaved aggressively.

Think about times at home/work when other people behaved aggressively towards you.

Do you want to change anything about your behaviour?

Passive behaviour is...

Keeping quiet for fear of upsetting people
Avoiding conflict
Saying yes when you want to say no
Always putting other people's needs first
Not expressing your feelings
Going along with thing you don't like or agree with
Apologising excessively
Inwardly burning with anger and frustration
Being vague about your ideas and what you want
Justifying your actions to other people
Appearing indecisive

"The duty we owe ourselves is greater than that we owe others."

Louisa May Alcott

Have you ever found yourself doing any of these things? Perhaps, like me you might have resorted to passive behaviour to keep the peace. Perhaps, you may have reached the point where you no longer know what your views or feelings are on a topic, even then, you'll probably notice a feeling of unease at being taken for granted or not being taken seriously. Passive behaviour is caused by a lack of confidence. If you can turn passive behaviour into assertive behaviour, it will boost your confidence.

Think about times at home/work when you behaved passively.

Think about times at home/work when you experienced someone behaving passively towards you.

Do you want to change anything about your behaviour?

Assertiveness is about building your self-respect

Assertive behaviour is…

Being open and honest with yourself and other people
Listening to other people's points of view
Showing understanding of other people's situations
Expressing your ideas clearly but not at the expense of others
Being able to reach workable solutions to difficulties
Making decisions, even if your decision is not to decide!
Being clear about your point and not getting side-tracked
Dealing with conflict
Having self-respect and respect for other people
Being equal with others and retaining your uniqueness
Expressing feelings honestly and with care

How often are you genuinely assertive? You might find that you are assertive in some situations, aggressive or passive in others.

Assertiveness is about respecting other people

Use the following questionnaire to work out your assertiveness level. Circle the a, b, c, or d response to see how you tend to behave in these situations. Work through the questionnaire quickly. Your first answers are usually the most accurate.

1. **You want to have Christmas or a similar festival with your partner/friend. They want to go to their family. Do you:**
   a) Imply that it's unfair and hope things will change
   b) Go to the family – anything for peace!
   c) Say how you feel and what you would like
   d) Flatly refuse to go

Assertiveness audit

Photo: Julia Caesar, Unsplash

2. **When a friend or colleague borrows your calculator regularly and forgets to return it to you, do you:**
   a) Drop hints at regular intervals
   b) Let it go
   c) Explain the effect on you and ask for it back
   d) Get angry and demand it back

3. **An interview panel member asks a question that seems sexist to you. Do you:**
   a) Quip back a quick retort
   b) Answer as best you can
   c) Express some concern about the question only if you feel OK about it
   d) Point out how wrong it is to ask such questions and refuse to answer

4. **When you are entering a car park and are about to reverse into a parking space another driver nips in and pinches the space. Do you:**
   a) Block the car in
   b) Ignore it and find another space
   c) Tell the other driver how annoyed you are and ask them to move
   d) Give the other driver a piece of your mind for their rudeness

5. **When someone criticises your appearance, do you:**
   a) Say something like "Well it's my most expensive outfit"
   b) Blush and say nothing
   c) Check what is specifically being said and judge for yourself
   d) Tell them it's none of their business

6. **You are asked to work late for the third time this week. You already have another appointment. Do you:**
   a) Give what you think is a cast-iron reason for not staying
   b) Try to say 'no' and end up staying
   c) Say 'no' firmly and say when you need to leave for your appointment
   d) Complain it's the third time this week and say a definite 'no'

7. **Members of your family don't seem to be listening when you try telling them about your plans for Saturday. Do you:**
   a) Say something like "Well it anyone's interested I'm..."
   b) Keep quiet
   c) Say how you feel and that it's important for you to tell them about your plans
   d) Talk more loudly

8. **When you keep quiet in a situation, is it because:**
   a) You know the silence will have an effect
   b) You are too upset or frightened to speak
   c) You have nothing to say
   d) You're sulking

9. **When you feel angry or upset, do you:**
   a) Let people know in a roundabout way
   b) Keep quiet
   c) Try to say how you feel and be specific
   d) Explode

Count how many As, Bs, Cs and Ds you've scored

A	B	C	D

Mostly Bs

Your behaviour tends to be passive.

Mostly Cs

This shows that you tend to be assertive but check that you genuinely do the things you say you do. It is easy to see what the best solution is on paper, but a more passive or more aggressive response may slip out in the heat of the moment.

Mostly As and Ds

Your behaviour tends to be aggressive. The Ds are directly aggressive, whilst the As are indirectly aggressive and manipulative. Most people confuse assertive behaviour with aggressive behaviour so it's not unusual to have a high score here.

What do you want to change about this pattern?

Have another look at your quiz answers. What are your:

Strengths	Challenges

How could these affect your career choices?

What potential barriers would stop you from acting assertively?

Have you ever experienced prejudice? If yes, how did you react?

Would you change your behaviour if you experienced prejudice again? If yes, what would you change?

Just remember...

Nobody's perfect! We both know that being assertive is easier when you're having a good day, even the most confident person struggles on bad days. But what's one day compared to the rest of your life? Do you remember the sunflowers I mentioned earlier? The days when you are feeling more vulnerable are the best days to turn to your friends and networks for support. Believe it or not, the sun will rise again tomorrow, a fresh new day, another chance for you to work on your confidence.

Celebrating difference

Stereotypes

No matter what your identity is, your age, gender, nationality, race, colour, faith, disability, neurodiversity, sexual orientation, or any other difference, we are all human beings trying to achieve security and happiness for ourselves and our families. In fact, difference makes it possible for you to contribute something that another person could not.

Please give 3 examples of stereotypes:

1

2

3

Now, can you find at least one advantage to an employer/the workplace for each of the stereotypes that you listed above? For example, if you gave the stereotype of an employer worrying about promoting a woman in her 40s to a senior position you could mention the experience and skills that she would bring to the role (e.g. consistency), her age would make it highly unlikely that she will later take several years off to raise a young family. A second advantage could be her experience, this would make her great at problem solving because she has probably encountered a situation in the past and observed others solving it.

1

2

3

And breathe...

You'll be delighted to know that you've just finished all the personal diagnostics! Very Well Done!! Now please take a break and reward yourself. It might be a piping hot mug of tea and a cheeky bar of chocolate; whatever it is, you have well and truly earned it, enjoy :o)

Review

Update your logbook

Please check that you have finished these activities:

Tree of Life (jelly babies)
Personal Development Plan
Values elucidation
Self-esteem audit
Assertiveness audit
Celebrating difference

Reflective diary

How do your personal values and self-esteem affect planning goals for your future? Prepare a short reflective paragraph for your diary. Please make an audio recording of this paragraph.

Forget-me-nots

It is said that in the beginning, the Creator took great delight in decorating flowers. Waiting patiently until the end, was a cluster of tiny flowers. "What about me?" squeaked one of the flowers, its head drooping, "The Almighty in your mercy, loves wonderous diversity. Alas, all the colours have been used to decorate the bigger flowers, what is left for me?" The Creator gazed at the crestfallen little flower, "Beloved, I have reserved the best for you, you will be the rarest of colours amongst flowers. For you will be bathed in blue from the heavens. Your head will no longer droop but joyfully face the skies. Gold from the sun will sparkle in the heart of your bloom, for the Creator forgot you not".

Today, forget-me-nots are loved for their perky little sky-blue flowers... Just imagine if one of these wildflowers decided to reflect the pink of the evening sky for a change.

Photo: Mariya Mammiya, Pixabay

Chapter 2

"Challenges are what make life interesting and overcoming them is what makes life meaningful."

Joshua J Marine

What are your 3 secret weapons?

Now that we know more about who you are, let's look at what skills you could exchange for the money and status you want. In Chapter 1, the diagnostics were designed to find out all about you as a person… and you sailed through those, right? ;o)

In this chapter, the diagnostics are all about what skills you bring to the workplace. You'll identify your strengths and challenges; look at your personal power/influence; map your skills to an employer's needs; identify any gaps, set yourself some SMART goals and create an action plan for your job search. No this isn't easy, but the strategic approach will give you an unfair advantage later when it comes to writing interview-guaranteeing CVs.

SWOT analysis

Strengths, Weaknesses, Opportunities, Threats

What personal strengths or skills do you have? Don't be shy, what are you good at or feel particularly proud of…?

Could you give me at least one example from the workplace where you saved an employer/company either time or money? Describe what happened:

"Miracles happen to those who believe in them."

Bernhard Berenson

Did you get any support from an individual or a network to help you to achieve your success(es)? If yes, please list them:

What are your challenges or weaknesses? Obviously jot down whatever you want here but don't be too hard on yourself, **this list should not be longer than your strengths**!

What opportunities are available to you? These could be paid work, promotion, charity or volunteering, retraining, something else that you've always wanted to do…

What threats do you face? What are you most afraid of?

Transferable skills

Now take a moment to flick back to your personal strengths, skills, and values that you listed in Chapter 1. Could any of them be transferred to the workplace? Could any of them be the foundation of further successes? If yes, please make a note of them here...

Photo: Tania Moushino, Unsplash

Personal power and influence

Think about a leader, manager, employer, or someone who has inspired you. Make a list of the things they did that:

Built trust

Challenged you

What were the results? How was your/others' performance affected? How did you feel?

What could you do tomorrow to build trust?

What could you do to challenge yourself/others?

How could you improve your performance & confidence?

Matching your skills to employer needs

"If you want happiness for an hour, take a nap. If you want happiness for a day, go fishing. If you want happiness for a year, inherit a fortune. If you want happiness for a lifetime, help someone else."

Chinese proverb

There are some skills and qualifications that employers look for no matter what type of job they are offering. These include:

Ability to work on own initiative
Ability to work with a happy and friendly team
Achiever
Adaptable
Ambitious
Committed
Computer literate / good ITC / computer skills
Creative /creative flair
Cultural awareness
Current first aid certificate
Drive
Dynamic
Energy
Enthusiastic
Exceptional telephone manner
Experience / experience working with children
First class organisational skills
Full clean driving licence / own transport

Good attention to detail
Good communicator / good communication skills
Good team player
Information technology
Inter-personal skills
Knowledge of software
Manage resources
Managerial / supervisory qualification /
Methodical – follow through
Motivated / motivator
Non-judgemental
Numerate
Professional
Provide quality service
Reliable
Sensitive to needs of others
Smart
Strategic vision
Strong leadership skills
Strong administrative skills

Workplace skills

- Please put a tick against any item on the list above if you have that skill or qualification.
- How many of these skills or qualifications do you have?
- Can you add any more skills or qualifications to this list?

"If you don't like something, change it. If you can't change it, change the way you think about it."
Mary Engelbreit

Photo: Wolfilser, Shuttershock

29

Skills audits

Local skills audit

Which skills, qualities or qualifications are needed in your local area? You could look through council publications, social media

Skills	Qualities	Qualifications

National skills audit

Which skills, qualities and qualifications are needed nationally? You could do some online research about national shortages.

Skills	Qualities	Qualifications

International skills audit

Now working from home is more of a thing globally, you might want to include an international skills audit in this exercise.

Skills	Qualities	Qualifications

Which of your personal skills or strengths match these needs?

Skills	Qualities	Qualifications

Skills gap analysis

Compare your local/national/international skills audit with your personal skills analysis. Are there any gaps between your current skills or knowledge and those you need for your chosen career objectives? If there are, please make a note of them here...

Personal skills analysis

"Why are you the best person for the job?"

What are the top 3 skills that you have to offer? They could be skills, achievements, or qualifications that you are proud of. Use the following table to:

- Describe your skills or qualifications
- Identify any areas you need to polish

Strength/skill	Already have	Need to polish
Strength/skill 1 Relevant experience, something you are proud of, or other people often compliment you on		
Strength/skill 2		
Strength/skill 3		
Additional experience What other strengths can you bring to a job, e.g., what skills did you learn from raising a family?		
Qualifications What do you already have? Do you need any more to get the career you really want?		

Goal setting

Achieving Goals

Goal setting helps to

Give you a clear direction and purpose
Prioritise and choose what you want to do
Decide what form of success will suit you and your circumstances
Measure how you are progressing against your goals
Evaluate what adjustments you need to make when, where and how to achieve your targets
Decide if you need to change your goals or tactics if there is a change in circumstances

SMART goals

One of the most effective ways of setting goals is to use the SMART system. SMART stands for:

Specific   Measurable   Achievable   Realistic   Targeted

Be Specific

Specify what you will achieve and by what date.

Measure success

How will you know when you have succeeded? What measures will be used and where will feedback come from?

Set Achievable goals

Create mini goals along the way to review progress, build on success, learn from failure, and get early benefits.

Be Realistic

Goals should be challenging but achievable. They should take risks and constraints into account.

Be Targeted

Focus on priorities, don't waste time and effort on things that generate little or low value rewards.

Goal suggestions for action plans

Use your failures
Challenge your fears
Use healthy thinking
Build your self-esteem
Challenge your limiting beliefs
Make changes in your roles
Use role models
Learn from others
Feel good about yourself
Sound more confident

So, what's **your** plan?

Now that you have a clear idea of what skills you have to offer and where the gaps are, if any, do you have any goals that you want to set yourself to make the most of the opportunities available? Are there any skills that you have always wanted to learn but haven't yet had a chance to?

My personal goals are:

1

2

3

What do I need to do to achieve these goals?

Your SMART goal

Photo: Ken Cheung

Now pick one of those personal goals to look at in detail

Your **specific** personal goal is:

You will know that you are succeeding because you have set the following **measurements**:

Your goal is **achievable** because

Photo: Chungkuk Bae, Unsplash

"Everyone has something to contribute to this world. It's just a matter of being given that opportunity to do so."

Grace Hightower

Pause and reflect

Action plans

"Nothing can dim the light which shines from within."

Maya Angelou

"We must not be beggars. Why should we beg when we have something to offer"

Ziaur Rahman

Your goal is realistic, you have considered the following risks:

Your goal is targeted. You are focusing on:

"Each of us brings to the world unique talents, gifts and abilities. Even if you don't know what it is or value what you do, someone, somewhere will benefit from your presence. No one can do what you do exactly the way you do it. It is this uniqueness that makes you valuable to the world. We are each as unique and valuable as the other. It was designed that way. A gift from God. Gifts are not given on the basis of race or gender. As a matter of truth, gifts come in many shapes, sizes and colours. When you do what you do, exactly the way you do it, you are sharing God's gifts, bestowed for the good of the world."

Maya Angelou

Silently repeat the following phrase to yourself 3 times:

I have a valuable gift to share with the world.

5 steps to create an action plan...

Step 1
Imagine that you have achieved a specific goal. How do you know that you have achieved it?

Step 2
Working backwards, identify the action and mini goals you need to enable you to get there.

Step 3
Identify any support and feedback you will need and what you need to do to receive it.

Step 4
Identify any obstacles. How will you overcome them?

Step 5
Get someone to look at your plan and give you feedback.

Personal Action Plan

Photo: Joanna Kosinski, Unsplash

"If it ain't broke, don't fix it"
Thomas Bertram Lance

Step 1

Just imagine that you have achieved a specific goal. How do you know that you have achieved it?

Step 2

Working backwards, please list the actions and mini goals you would need to enable you to get there.

Step 3

What support and/or feedback will you need and what do you need to do to get it?

Step 4

Can you think of any obstacles? How will you overcome them?

Step 5

Get someone to look at your plan and give their feedback.

"Weaknesses are just strengths in the wrong environment."
Marianne Cantwell

Review

"Everything has beauty, but not everyone sees it."

Confucius

Update your logbook

Please make sure that you have finished the following activities for your logbook:

SWOT analysis
Personal power and influence
Workplace skills
Skills audit
Personal skills analysis
Gap analysis
Personal action plan

Reflective diary

What 3 skills or experiences are you most proud of and why?

1

2

3

Write an entry for your reflective diary. If you are building an audio recording, please record your reflective diary entry.

"We think sometimes that poverty is only being hungry, naked and homeless. The poverty of being unwanted, unloved and uncared for is the greatest poverty."

Mother Theresa

Chapter 3

Photo: Simone Dalmeri, Unsplash

"Keep your face always toward the sunshine, and shadows will fall behind you."
Walt Whitman

THE Top Secret of Success

And now for the very heart of this book

There's a very good reason why banks, funders and mentors ask prospective new businesses to write a business plan. Most new businesses will fail. The ones that have a clear plan, strategic objectives and financial forecasts are far more likely to succeed. It's a bit unorthodox but I'm recommending that you write a business plan for your dream lifestyle. Don't roll your eyes at me like that please! I will help you to do it.

Creating a treasure map

Most good business plans have an executive summary at the front. This is usually written once the business plan is finished but, in our case, you and I will create a graphic executive summary, I call it the treasure map to your dream.

I need you to be totally honest about what you really want and what you don't. You will use tools to chart your map in detail, warts, and all. Then we will both spend the rest of this journey turning your personal business plan into reality. By the time you have finished, you will have a blueprint to take you from where you are today to your perfect life. You will also have a financial forecast with a clear idea of how much you need to earn now and how much you need in the future to fund your perfect life.

First gather some key materials

You can make your map as simple or as elaborate as you like. Think of somewhere safe to store it so that you can keep going back to it and update your progress during your journey. Your map can be your secret document hidden away from prying eyes or a piece of art in progress, proudly displayed in your home while you are working on it.

To do this activity, you'll need:

A piece of blank flip-chart paper or card, A3 or larger **OR** use the blank pages at the back of this book **OR** create a virtual mood board online
A selection of colourful marker pens
A selection of pencils including colours
Prints/photos/magazine cuttings that illustrate aspects of your dream life
Prices for the products/items in your dream images
A selection of images or representations of things you want to remove from your life
Glue stick
Any additional stickers, sequins, paints, or embellishments
An open mind
A big smile :o)

"When you have a dream, you've got to grab it and never let go."
Carol Burnett

Your treasure map

So, what's on your map?

You are about to plot a path from where you are in your life right now to your perfect lifestyle. This might include strategic objectives for example you might need to take a course, workplace training or continuing professional development (CPD) to gain the skills you need for your dream position. Cut out or print images from magazines, the internet, job adverts etc. to describe elements on your map for example what would you like to do in your Me Time? Is there an image to show that activity?

Starting position

Pick a starting position anywhere on your blank canvas. Use an image, a photo, a diagram or even an "x" to show where you are in your life at this moment. Are there things in your life right now that you no longer want? Add words or images to describe them.

Goal

Then decide where to position your perfect life on the map. Use words and images to show what your dream looks like. You might have a beautiful home, a specific car, a particular job, whatever perfect means to you. Remember the values you listed in Chapter 1? Does your perfect life reflect them? If not, do you need to make some adjustments to your plan?

Life values

Next you need to add your life values more generally. These might be around your starting position, around your perfect life or sprinkled all over your map. Your values are what makes you, YOU. Are you honouring them in your current lifestyle? Would your perfect life work for them? How can you use them to help you to achieve your perfect lifestyle?

Achievements

Now it's time to add your skills and abilities, 3 reasons why you are the best person for the job. Where can you best deploy these to achieve your perfect life? Do you need to polish some? Is it worth taking a detour to do this? Can you get workplace training?

Opportunities

Have you achieved all the potential you can from your current job? Is there scope for promotion? Perhaps you could have a quiet chat with your line manager or Human Resources to make it clear that you are keen to progress and would like to be considered for promotion and/ or further training. Capture these thoughts/decisions on your map. Opportunities may not be immediately available. If you are aware of something in the pipeline, add it to your map as a strategic objective but a little distance away from your starting position.

Photo: Stephen Eickshen, Unsplash

"The kiss of the sun for pardon,
The song of the birds for mirth,
One is nearer God's Heart
* in a garden*
Then anywhere else on Earth."

Dorothy Frances Gurney

Recap

Reality check

"Do not dwell in the past,
do not dream of the future,
concentrate the mind on
the present moment."

Buddha

Me Time

Now for my favourite bit on the map, Me Time! For life to be perfect, you need quality time to yourself. What do you enjoy doing? Would you like to try something new? Perhaps weekends away, spa retreats? Whatever it is, please put it on your map, illustrate it with words and/or images to show how you would spend that precious time.

Life path

The final step (for now) is to plot a route from where you are today, through the various stages until you arrive at your dream life. This could be a simple black line; little footprints, shoe prints, arrows or whatever you like. The main thing is that you need to think hard and plan a realistic path including strategic objectives like training and sideways moves even a new job if that's what it takes to achieve your goal. It doesn't matter if you race along or travel at a more leisurely pace providing you make progress.

We both know that life rarely goes to plan, you might end up taking a diversion or completely different route. You might like to map the route you take in real life in a different way to the route that you planned to show how it differs from the original plan.

By the time you have finished, your map should have:

- Starting position
- Goal
- Personal (Life) values
- Achievements
- Opportunities
- Me time
- Life path

How much money do you need to earn?

Please bear in mind that **money is <u>not</u> the answer to everything**. If you spend it wisely, you might not need to earn as much as you think. What do you want the money for? Do you really need to pay for it in money? Could you pay for it with your time, skills, or talents instead? Could you do a favour to help a friend in exchange for help to achieve your goal or at least part of it?

Every resilient business plan needs a set of calculated financial forecasts and yours is no different. You need absolute clarity on what your existing budget is and how much you need to fund your future lifestyle. **It's time to get real about finance**.

You'll be delighted to hear that finance is a lot more interesting when it becomes a way of measuring progress. It's very much like keeping score in a game of Monopoly, or Monotony as my sister calls it! I'm guessing that you want Mayfair not Old Kent Road ;o)

Quick finance quiz

Before we start, please could you to do this little quiz? It will be interesting to see what your baseline reaction to money is before we explore some healthy financial habits. Please answer the following questions with:

Y = Yes   **N** = No   **N/S** = Not Sure   **N/A** = Not applicable

Money worries
Do you often worry about money?

Spending habits
Are you worried that your spending habits are putting the plans for your future at risk?

Managing money
Do you keep getting overdrawn on your bank account?

Do you only pay the minimum payments due on your loans and credit cards each month?

Have you checked that you're getting the best deal for your heating and lighting?

When you buy home or car insurance, do you renew with your existing company?

When you buy home or car insurance, do you shop around?

Money to pay your bills
Do you find that you sometimes need to borrow money from friends or family?

Are you paying your bills with money put aside for other things?

Saving for emergencies
Do you have any savings for a 'rainy day' or emergencies?

Cutting tax
Do you know how to reduce the tax on your savings?

Planning for your future
If you or your partner lost your job or couldn't work due to ill health, would you be in financial trouble straight away?

Interest rates
Do you know what interest rates you pay on loans, credit cards or your mortgage?

Do you know what interest rates you receive on any savings?

Photo: Maurizio Ciabatti, Shutterstock

Personal finance

My Mum used to say that "a donkey in her own kitchen is better than a genius in someone else's". Loosely translated from the Italian, this means that you don't need to be a genius to know your way around familiar territory. You probably already manage your finances beautifully. In which case perhaps you can compare your strategies with the ones that I'm about to mention. If, however, your system could do with a tweak, I hope you find at least some of my tips useful. By the way, I've never shared these secrets with anyone else before!

You and I experience life in a series of ebbs and flows. At high tide, we have money flooding in, there's too much work and not enough time to do it. At low tide, money is scarce, but we have all the time we need. Rather than being stressed at each stage, how about accepting that these are both natural parts of the cycle and use one to prepare for the other... radical! Use good times to put money aside for rainy days, use quieter days to plan for better times.

You and I live in very different circumstances. Challenges like being unemployed, a single parent or having a disability will obviously influence the way that you manage your finances. I've tried to keep my tips and templates general, but they might not all work for you. Use what you find useful and just note the rest.

Ruth's personal financial tips

Technology

Financial management apps

Obviously, there are loads of apps out there designed to help you manage your finances. I recommend Emma, which is registered with the Financial Conduct Authority, is designed for women, helps you set monthly budgets, recommends money saving comparisons, offers cashbacks, saving plans and even investment opportunities from £1 (you can buy a fraction of a share). Whether you go for one of the paid options, or the free version, this app does all the hard work for you, and you can manage all your finances in one place.

Smartphones

If you want to create your own budgeting system, I suggest you use the Notes app on your mobile phone so you can manage it wherever you happen to be. Plan at least one month in advance so you know when you need to save for an expensive week.

I suggest you list your monthly income and outgoings in weeks so you can make small adjustments and avoid feast or famine scenarios. Start by creating a heading for each week by start and end dates. That's 4–5 headings depending on how many weeks are in that month, e.g.: 3–9 January, 10–16 January, 17–23 January, 24–30 January.

Next, list your income and outgoings in date order under the relevant week, a few days before the payment is due. Prepare enough money in your account to cover each week's outgoings. This might mean sometimes keeping more money than you need in your account(s). Update your balances regularly, preferably every day, making little adjustments to your records if necessary.

Always check your weekly budget before spending any "spare" money, you might have been saving it for the following week!

Online banking

Use mobile banking apps to check your bank and credit card balances daily. Check for any unusual activity/fraud. Cross-reference the information with your weekly budget. Transfer any money that you are saving for another week into an instant access savings account if possible until you need it. The Emma app can make it so easy to do all this.

Credit score apps

Download a free credit score app like Clear Score to help you keep track of your credit rating. These apps usually have a coaching function that helps you to improve your rating. Check the information displayed about you each month for accuracy and report any corrections you need as they crop up.

Spreadsheets

Monthly spreadsheets are much easier to see on a laptop screen than mobile phone. These are great for doing the calculations for you, providing the formulae have been put in correctly(!) The information is essentially the same as the weekly budgets on your mobile phone, but it is easier to do long term planning, spot trends and measure your progress against your objectives. Make a list of your saving goals in priority order, then gradually incorporate them into your accounts as your finances improve.

Credit rating

Here are a few quick tips on improving your credit rating:
- Use a credit card little and often
- Keep credit utilisation low, never use more than 50%
- Fix mistakes on your report
- Get on the electoral register
- Don't make multiple credit applications at the same time
- Use an eligibility checker
- Get your name on some bills if it isn't already
- Pay your bills on time
- Look out for fraud
- Make sure you have a good overall view of your finances

Do you have any county court judgements (CCJs) or insolvency voluntary arrangements (IVAs)? **No is good.**

Are you on the electoral register? **Yes, is good**. How long have you had your bank account(s) for? **The longer, the better**.

What percentage of your credit limit(s) are you using? **Never** use more than 50% of your card's limit. Someone with a good credit rating will use their card(s) little and often, pay off their balance each month and avoid paying any fees.

Do you make your loan(s) repayments on time? Remember that your mobile phone contract counts as a loan. When paying back loans, try to make 2-3 monthly repayments on time then repay the rest of the loan off early in one go if your circumstances allow. This will turbo charge your credit rating. The easiest way to do this is to borrow a small amount when you don't need it, make 2-3 repayments then use the loan to repay the balance.

Repeat this process with a larger loan every 6 months until you have repaid a very large loan. Providing you follow the other tips in this credit rating section, repaying the loans on time and then early will give you/your business an excellent credit rating which should help you get finance in an emergency if you need it. Talking about loans, if your application for one is turned down, don't keep applying to other lenders. Every application generates a hard search on your credit file. A cluster of hard searches will make lenders think that you are struggling and are a bad risk.

Balance vs purchase credit cards

With so many types of credit cards out there, it can be hard to choose the right one for you. What you want to use it for? Do you want to spread the cost of a purchase? Save money on your credit card bill? Build your credit history?

Here is a simple guide to the main types of credit card to help you make an informed choice.

Credit builder cards

If you're looking for a credit score boost, a credit builder card could be for you. You don't need a high credit score to be accepted, and using one responsibly is a great way to boost your score.

Money transfer cards

Struggling with an expensive overdraft? A money transfer card lets you transfer money from your credit card straight into your bank account, so you can pay off your overdraft for less.

Purchase cards

If you're planning a big purchase, a purchase card can be a cheap way to borrow, they usually come with an interest-free period.

Rewards cards

Rewards cards reward you for using them. You might get travel miles, cashback, or store discounts. These cards usually charge an annual fee and have higher interest rates, so make sure the benefits outweigh the costs for you.

Shopping tips

Do your weekly shop online several days before you need the delivery so you can:

Book a delivery slot that suits you best

Review your trolley

Keep updating your trolley as you remember things

Set a budget and stick to it, adjust if you go over budget. If you have gone over budget, boost moral by keeping a few little luxuries and removing things that you won't miss e.g., remove 1 of the bottles of bleach you've ordered and buy a treat instead.

Buy a favourite thing for each member of the household.

Plan meals: veg to go with mains, meals to cook, portion, freeze

Buy ingredients to batch cook healthy meals and soups to freeze when you have time to cook

Set personal targets e.g., add more fruit and veg

Use up perishable items before fresh produce arrives.

Damage limitation

Protect yourself, your loved ones and assets with insurance policies including health, life, household, and pet insurance.

Most financial experts recommend that you need a cash reserve of at least 6 months' worth of expenses to support yourself in an emergency. If you need £3,000 to survive every month including mortgage, household bills etc. then you need to build up a safety net of £18,000. Personal finance guru Suze Orman recommends an 8-month emergency fund because that is how long it takes the average person to find a new job.

Debt management

Many of us use borrowing to manage our finances. But which is right for you, credit card or a loan? Credit cards are a good option if you want to save on interest, as many have 0% offers. The downside is you can't borrow more than your credit limit. If you're looking to borrow larger amounts, a loan could be right for you. Even though you'll pay interest, it can be a cost-effective way to borrow and even consolidate existing debts.

Don't bury your head in the sand, debt won't magically disappear on its own. I have included a financial statement template at the

"Our greatest glory is not in never falling, but in rising every time we fall."

Confucius

back of this book that you can fill in and use to negotiate a sensible repayment plan if you need to. Once you have made an agreement, **<u>stick to it</u>**. Use this as a way of learning how to save. Once you have repaid your debt(s), carry on putting a regular amount of money aside for a rainy day – we all get them.

The UK's leading debt charity, **StepChange** (0800 138 1111, https://www.stepchange.org), can offer free advice and a range of solutions to help you pay, manage, or write off your debt if you live in the UK. They can also give you a free personal action plan to deal with your debt. If you meet certain conditions, **StepChange** can also help you to apply for Breathing Space.

Officially, Breathing Space is called the Debt Respite Scheme. This is a UK government scheme to relieve some of the pressure caused by being in debt. For 60 days, you'll be protected from your creditors for the debts registered in your Breathing Space. During this time, you only pay what you can afford **but** any missed payments will go on your credit file and affect your credit rating. Breathing Space is available in England and Wales, Scotland has a similar Moratorium Period.

While you're on your 60-day Breathing Space, your creditors can't act against you for any listed Breathing Space debts you owe. No interest, fees or charges should be added to these debts, and your creditors should not send you any demands for payment, you might still get reminder letters though. In return you'll have a few obligations to prevent your protection from being cancelled:

- Make regular payments to your existing commitments e.g., your rent, mortgage, hire purchase and utility bills where you can
- Seek debt advice/continue your debt solution application
- Inform your debt advisor of any changes to your circumstances while you're on the scheme
- Don't take out more than £500 in additional credit, on your own or with anyone else.

Once your 60-day Breathing Space is up, you can't apply for another one for 12 months even if you haven't finished setting up your debt solution. You'll still need to make repayments for the debts that were listed in your original application if you can afford to so it's important to set up an affordable debt solution while you're on Breathing Space.

Once your Breathing Space has ended, your creditors can:

- Start applying interest, charges, fees, and penalties to your debt from the date it ended. However, these can't be backdated without a court order.
- Start contacting you again and trying to reclaim the debt.
- Start or resume court action to reclaim the debt

"Hard work keeps the wrinkles out of the mind and spirit."

Helena Rubinstein

However, if you've started an affordable debt solution, or made a formal arrangement with your creditors to repay your debt, this could stop or reduce the above actions being taken.

Savings

Plan to save but be realistic, you don't need to cripple yourself by squirreling every 'spare' penny. Great oaks from little acorns grow. Even £30 a month quickly builds up into a useful amount. Be aware that banks have maximum limits to what they must repay if they go bankrupt. **This total can be spread across different branches and brand names owned by the same bank**. Check the terms and conditions of your bank, make sure that the combined total you have in all the different accounts you have with that bank is safely under its legal limit. There are lots of ways for you to save including: shares, bonds, investments, antiques, collectibles, and art. Perhaps you could commission a new piece of art?

Your notes

Photo: Faye Cornish, Unsplash

Your Personal Business Plan

Don't let the words "business plan" worry you. This one will give you clarity on what you need to do to achieve your goals. You can avoid making expensive mistakes by adjusting it now. I hope that you'll find it useful to think about your life options in this way. Feel free to photocopy, photograph or scan this plan to show to your bank manager or potential funder.

I have given you a few prompts to help you fill in each section. Please don't feel that you need to write loads, If the question can be answered in one sentence, don't waste time writing more.

Job title
What kind of role/position are you looking for?

Nature of business
What kind of work do you do?

Market sector
What sector do you want to work in e.g., education, finance?

Do some online research on current trends in that market sector:

How much is it worth a year to the national/global economy?
Where is demand, rising or falling?
What are the emerging trends?
Can you spot trends that you can take advantage of?

Strategic objectives

What are the key stages that you've listed on your treasure map?
How will your new job/business help you to achieve these?
How long do you think each stage will take roughly?

Market

What kind of organisation do you want to work in? A small, local company? A multibillion international corporation? A charity? Your own consultancy etc.?
Can you earn the amount you need to fund your perfect life in this size/type of organisation?

Networks

Do you have a network of contacts you could collaborate with?
What relevant skills do you and your network have between you?

Profile

Why have you made this career choice? What is the back story?

Offering

Is the work you do essential/key worker or nice to have?
Why? What evidence/research do you have to back this up?
What exactly are you offering? A product, service, other?
Do you have a follow-up offer(s)? Perhaps optional extras?

Pricing policy

Are you asking for the market rate, above this rate or below?
How can you justify your target earnings/prices?

Competitive edge

List 3 reasons why you are the best person for the job/role
1

2

3

Typical customers

Look back at the market research that you did earlier.
Who/what are the most profitable areas to target?
Why are you targeting these organisations/customers?
Are you working with similar organisations/customers now?

Earnings forecast

Your anticipated earnings for Year 1 = £

Your anticipated earnings for Year 2 = £

Your anticipated earnings for Year 3 = £

Your anticipated earnings for Year 4 = £

Your anticipated earnings for Year 5 = £

Funding requirement

Do you need to pay for anything before you can start making
money? For example, do you need additional training, specialist
equipment, clothing? How will you fund these expenses?

Exit strategy

How long do you plan to stay in this new role for?
What do you need to achieve in this time?
Do you think you will move to a different company?
Would you be interested in merging with another company?
Would you be interested in taking over another company?
What do you need to do to get ready for the next stage?

Templates

Review

There are some useful templates for you at the back of this book including a financial planner to make a repayment plan and a forward planner to jot down your goals. If it would make your life easier to use spreadsheets that do the calculations for you, please email hello@ instantimpact.org and I'll send those to you.

Update your logbook

Please make sure that you have finished the following for your logbook:

Treasure Map
Quick finance quiz
Your Personal Business Plan

Reflective diary

What one thing could you do today to reduce the risks to your personal finances? Write an entry for your reflective diary. If you are building an audio recording of this journey, please record your reflective diary entry.

Chapter 4

"The roots of education are bitter, but the fruit is sweet."
Aristotle

Secret of Success 2

Now that you have the clarity of a personal business plan, it's time to look at the figures. In Chapter 4, I will help you to do a financial audit before preparing your financial forecasts. The audit will give you a clearer idea of what you are spending now so you can adjust it if you need to. The financial forecasts will help you to measure your success against your business plan objectives as you progress towards your goals.

Personal finance audit

Please complete the audit below. It's your choice which column you use week, month, or quarter, but be consistent and only use **one** of the three.

Income			
Income	Weekly £	Monthly £	Quarterly £
Wages/salary/pension			
Benefits			
Contributions			
Maintenance			
Student loan			
Other			
Other			
Total income			
Outgoings			
Household	Weekly £	Monthly £	Quarterly £
Rent or Mortgage			
Building insurance			
Contents insurance			
Council tax			
Heating			
Lighting			
Water			
Telephone			
TV licence			
Repairs/renewals			
Other			
Other			
Total household			

Food & clothes	Weekly £	Monthly £	Quarterly £
Food and groceries			
Work lunches			
School lunches			
School uniforms			
Children's shoes			
Clothes/shoes, self			
Clothes/shoes, partner			
Casual clothes, children			
Other			
Other			
Total food & clothes			
Travel	Weekly £	Monthly £	Quarterly £
Adult fares			
Children's fares			
Car insurance			
Car servicing			
Car tax			
Fuel			
Visits to friends/relatives			
Other			
Other			
Total travel			
Finance	Weekly £	Monthly £	Quarterly £
Bank charges			
Credit card 1			
Credit card 2			
Loan repayments			
Pension contribution			
Storecard			
Other			
Other			
Total finance			
Other	Weekly £	Monthly £	Quarterly £
Alcohol			
Birthday presents			
Child/spouse maintenance			

Christmas presents			
Cigarettes			
Holidays			
Life insurance			
Meals/drinks out			
Newspapers/magazines			
Prescriptions			
Savings			
Subscriptions			
University/college fees			
Other			
Other			
Total other			

Summary of outgoings			
Outgoings	**Weekly £**	**Monthly £**	**Quarterly £**
Home			
Food & clothes			
Travel			
Finance			
Other			
Other			
Total outgoings			

Final balance			
Totals	**Weekly £**	**Monthly £**	**Quarterly £**
Total income			
Minus total outgoings			
Balance			

Cashflow forecasts

You may already know that cashflow forecasts are used to assess your ability to repay a loan. In this case, we are using one to check how realistic your business plan is. As your goal, your perfect future, is so precious I suggest that you use realistic, if not pessimistic figures.

Cashflow forecast terms
A quick reminder before we start:
Total income – total income you expect for the month
Total payments – total expected payments for the month
Opening balance – bank balance at the beginning of the month
Closing balance – bank balance at the end of the month.

"Failure is the condiment that gives success its flavor."
Truman Capote

Personal cashflow forecast (months 1–6)

This table will help you create your personal cashflow forecast. You might want to photocopy it to use over several years. If you would prefer to use spreadsheets that do the calculations for you, please email hello@instantimpact.org

Year	Month						Total
20___	1	2	3	4	5	6	£
Income							
Total income							
Outgoings							
Total outgoings							
Opening balance							
+ income							
– outgoings							
Closing balance							

Personal cashflow forecast (months 7–12)

This table will help you create your personal cashflow forecast. You might want to photocopy it to use over several years. If you would prefer to use spreadsheets that do the calculations for you, please email hello@instantimpact.org

Year	7	8	9	10	11	12	Total
20___							£
Income							
Total income							
Outgoings							
Total outgoings							
Opening balance							
+ income							
- outgoings							
Closing balance							

Review

Update your logbook

Please make sure that you have finished the following for your logbook:

Personal finance audit
Personal cashflow forecasts

Reflective diary

Now that you have had a good look at your finances, do you need to make tweaks to your personal business plan? Write an entry for your reflective diary. If you are making an audio recording of this journey, record your reflective diary entry.

Yet we are the movers and shakers
Of the world for ever, it seems.

"Ode" from *Music & Moonlight*
Arthur William Edgar O'Shaughnessy

Photo: Richard Ion

Chapter 5

"Proper planning and preparation prevent p**s poor performance"
The British Army

You guessed it ... Secret of Success 3

You and I both know how nerve-wracking change can be. It's so much easier to put up with the familiar even if you hate it. Yes, the unknown can be daunting but how many times have you hesitated about doing something and then, once you've done it, wondered why you didn't do it ages ago?

In this chapter you'll clarify what kind of work you really want, start a scrapbook of job adverts, and create a job search planner with contact details to keep your research more focused.

Although you can do a lot of this work with a pen and paper, you will get a richer experience and much better results if you use whatever ICT technology you have access to.

Quick Quiz

What skills have you used in the past to search for jobs?

When was the last time you used these skills?

What happened the last time you looked for a job?

"You can only become truly accomplished at something you love. Don't make money your goal. Instead, pursue the things you love doing, and then do them so well that people can't take their eyes off you."
Maya Angelou

59

Preparing for the recruitment process

Accessing information

The digital age

You don't need me to tell you how much the world of work has changed over the past 30 years. The introduction of the internet, computer and mobile technology has completely revolutionised how we work. Changes in working patterns including flexible working, zero hours contracts, hot desking and working from home have further affected the workplace.

Whilst technology is great for planning and displaying data in different formats to suit the receiver's needs, you almost certainly have at least one tale to tell of a time when your computer crashed, perhaps you sent an email or text to the wrong person. Am I right?! Some people have even been sacked because of content they posted on social media. The lines between your personal and professional lives have blurred.

Do any of these workplace changes impact on your job search?

Can you please list how they would affect you personally?

Positive effects	Negative effects

Technology is great for

- Researching contact details of support groups
- Saving data including text, images, links, and information that would be of personal use/interest to you
- Researching online job adverts
- Printing job adverts to create a scrapbook
- Creating information maps

Optimising opportunities

How can jobs be stepping-stones to other opportunities?

"By doing, you become employable. It doesn't matter what the job is; by working, you learn new things, meet new people and are exposed to new ideas."

Kate Reardon

Support networks

You can use several different sources of information to look for jobs. Can you add a few more ideas to this list:

Apps   Networks
Associations   Newspapers
Family/Friends   Radio
Internet   Self (new business)
Jobcentre   Social media
Magazines   Specialist publications

Jobs scrapbook

Job adverts

Start collecting a scrapbook of your shortlisted job adverts. It's up to you what you put your clippings into as long as it keeps them safe. It would be useful to write the name and date of the publication they appeared in on the back of the cutting, print out, etc., you might need this information later.

Adverts analysis

"Starting a new job can be nerve-racking, but it's also exciting. You're embarking on a new future, positioning yourself to write a fresh story on a clean slate."

Adena Friedman

What impression are the job adverts giving you?
How does the job advert make you feel about the recruiter?
How are they influencing the recruitment market?
What message do they carry about identity, gender, age etc?

Use the template on page 63r to create a Job Search Planner that keeps your job hunt more focused.

Job Search planner

Information maps

Information maps are useful for keeping the key information you need in one place. This is the perfect place to save the contact details of support networks for your job search. I've put a blank Job Search template on the next page so you can photocopy it as many times as you need.

Key information to include:

Date, are your contacts current?
Personal contact(s)
Organisations
Networks
Specific names
Job titles
Addresses
Telephone numbers
Email addresses
Internet links/addresses
Best/preferred method of communication (best contact method)
Images/adverts – where and when did you find the information?
Additional information or notes including deadlines.

Update your planners to keep your search on track.

Your notes

Job Search planner

Date	Contact(s)	Name	Job title	Address	Phone	Email/web	Best contact method	Image/advert	Notes

Additional notes

Creating a career plan

Photo: Jeremy Bishop, Unsplash

"If opportunity doesn't knock, build a door."
Milton Berle

Your career planner

What kind of job do you really want?

The information you wrote in your Personal Development Plan, Personal Skills Audit and Personal Action Plan should give you a good idea of the kind of work that you would enjoy best. As you begin to look at your options, make a shortlist of opportunities that appeal to you, even if you don't have the required experience or qualifications now.

Good questions to ask yourself

Do you like the type of work?
Does the job fit in with your Personal Development Plan?
Will it provide you with the skills that you need for the future?
Is there scope for further professional development?
Can you live on the money?
Is it easy to travel to?
Do you need special clothing?
Can you see yourself working there for 2–3 years?

Your shortlist of job opportunities

1

2

3

4

5

What appeals to you about each one?

1

2

3

4

5

Can you spot a growing trend?

"Do not be too timid and squeamish about your actions. All life is an experiment."
Ralph Waldo Emerson

Could you introduce any of these features into your existing role? If yes, which ones?

Can you see any of these features in jobs that you are already qualified for? If yes, which ones?

Are there any gaps? If yes, how are you going to fill them?

Replying to job adverts

Send your email, letter, or application to a named individual wherever possible. This information is often carried in the job advert but it if isn't, contact the company, explain that you are about to apply for a job and need the name and job title of the person to whom you should address it.

If you are applying online or by email, create a document that you can update, copy, and paste from. It's more professional to save the final version in a .PDF format before uploading or sending it. If your application is handwritten, plan your answers on a notes app, your smartphone or rough paper first before copying it out in clear legible writing. Always use crisp white envelopes, if possible, if replying by post.

Dealing with nerves

It's all very well making plans and getting organised, but you still need courage to act. You wouldn't be human if you didn't have the occasional wobble of nerves or self-doubt. Everyone feels nervous before an interview. A touch of nerves usually helps you give a better performance. Here are a few suggestions to help you manage them:

Physical exercises

On your way to the interview (if you are not driving) or in the waiting room, clench your fists, screw up your face, clam your jaw, curl your toes and tighten your buttocks as hard as you can for a count of 5 then relax slowly. Repeat this routine 3 times. You could also try shaking your arms and hands by your sides to relax them. Sit squarely in your seat during your interview to avoid nervous twitches.

Breathing exercises

Deep breathing exercises can help to unlock your vocal cords. Take a deep breath through your mouth, hold it steady for a count of 5, then breathe out slowly through your nose. You could also try blowing hard a few times aiming at an imaginary cobweb in a far distant corner... do this when you are alone, so you don't look like a complete and utter prat whilst you do it! ;o)

I'll share more handy tips for dealing with interview nerves in **Making a BIG Splash**, but for now, you might find it useful to reflect on the words of the poem **Caged Bird** by Maya Angelou. This poem contrasts two birds, one wild, the other caged. Despite the oppression, the caged bird still has a song of freedom in its heart. Are you dreaming of freedom but trapped by your fear?

*"The caged bird sings
with a fearful trill
of things unknown
but longed for still
and his tune is heard
on the distant hill
for the caged bird
sings of freedom."*
Maya Angelou

"Caged Bird" from *Shaker, Why Don't You Sing?*

Silently repeat the following phrase to yourself 3 times:

I can do this, I <u>truly</u> can

And if you're a very clever clogs, you'll know that females from only 40% of northern European bird species sing (only roosters crow), but this poem is still a great metaphor! :o)

Review

Update your logbook

Please make sure that you have finished the following:

Your Job Search planner with contact details of support networks
Your career planner with a shortlist of job opportunities
Also, you'll probably need to update your treasure map

Reflective diary

Look at 2–3 of your career planner opportunities. What do they say about you? Write an entry for your reflective diary. If you are building an audio recording of this journey, please record your reflective diary entry.

Chapter 6

The art of persuasion

How would you describe the communication process in your own words? In this chapter, I'll quickly run through it before asking you to think about barriers to confident communication and how they can they be overcome. You'll then need to ask a friend to help you experience the affects that tone of voice and body language can have on confident communication.

There will be more focussed information about communication skills in the next 2 (optional) books in this trilogy. In **Strategic CV**s, I'll show you how to write a CV that guarantees an interview in 30 seconds, using key information that you have already created in this book! :o) In **Making a BIG Splash!** I'll teach you how to outperform other interview applicants, set a trap for the recruiters and negotiate a salary increase before you even start your new position.

The communication cycle

For real communication to take place, someone, "**a sender**", must try to communicate something, "**a message**", e.g., a piece of information, an idea, or a request to "**a receiver**", another person to whom the information is directed.

encoding   decoding

SENDER   ⇒   MESSAGE   ⇒   RECEIVER

transmit   receive

For meaningful communication to take place, the sender needs some form of feedback from the receiver to check that the message was received correctly.

encoding   decoding

SENDER   ⇒   MESSAGE   ⇒   RECEIVER

transmit   receive

FEEDBACK

What is confidence?

Thinking with Confidence

Things that **happen inside you** impact on your confidence and affect:

How you think and feel
How you play roles
Your personality
Your ambition
Your ability to get in touch with your real self

Speaking with confidence

Confidence affects the way you communicate:

How you talk
Your assertiveness
Building relationships
Influencing others
Dealing with conflict
Controlling the effects of stress

Projecting confidence

We use confidence to impress others by:

Appearing confident
Appearing professional at work
Spreading confidence to inspire / encourage others

Barriers to confident communication

Please could you list 3 strategies in the table below that can overcome barriers to confident communication. Then tell me what the strengths and weaknesses of each strategy are.

	Strategies	Strengths	Weaknesses
1			
2			
3			

Effective communication channels

You can choose to communicate verbally or non-verbally:

Verbal communication (aural)

In a casual conversation
In a pre-arranged conversation
In a large, small, formal, or informal meeting
In a presentation
By telephone
By social media e.g., FaceTime, Twitter, WhatsApp etc.
By videoconferencing

Non-verbal communication (not aural)

By email, text, another digital format
In a letter
In a memo
In a notice on a notice board
In a report
In an internal newsletter
In a brochure or other published literature
Diagrams, plans, charts, illustrations, and maps

Body language

You will need another person to help you to practice using verbal and non-verbal signals. Take turns at talking about any topic you like. The person who is listening needs to achieve 3 objectives:

1. You are really interested in what the other person is saying
2. Change the subject to another topic
3. You are totally bored with listening to the other person

Take turns at listening and speaking, ask yourself: How did it feel to be on the receiving end of these signals?

Which techniques were most effective?

Which techniques did you feel most comfortable using, why?

Review

Update your logbook

Please make sure that you have finished the following:

- Barriers to confident communication
- Body language

Reflective diary

What 3 key things did you learn working through this chapter? Write an entry for your reflective diary. If you are building an audio recording of this journey, please record your reflective diary entry.

Photo: "Cygnet" by Richard Ion

Conclusion

Photo: Bessi Hamiti, Pixabay

"The dandelion doesn't care what others see. It says, 'One day, they'll be making wishes upon me'."

B Atkinson
The Peaceful Achiever

"We keep moving forward, opening new doors, and doing new things, because we're curious and curiosity keeps leading us down new paths."
Walt Disney

The cherry on top

You've passed with flying colours!

Guess what? You had what it takes to get that promotion, new job or whatever your personal goal is from the very beginning! You didn't need to plough through this book to qualify to change your life. **What you needed was the sense of achievement**.

The process of creating a business plan for your dreams will have made you more self-aware, turbo charged your confidence and boosted your self-esteem. They will have reminded you just how great you are and what potential you have.

So, what's your unfair advantage?

There's no denying that this journey has been hard work but now the fun really starts. I keep mentioning your unfair advantage, but what exactly is it? It's the bank of precious personal information you have created in this logbook. Your thinking, your personal traits and other great stuff. I can almost guarantee that most other women wouldn't have put in this much effort.

You have the clarity to choose the right career options for your authentic self, and strategic content to make your CV stand out from the crowd. **You have made life so much easier for yourself**.

Next steps

You have a business plan and financial forecasts to take you from wherever you are in your life to your perfect lifestyle. So, where do you go from here? You put your hard-won knowledge to good use and start making those changes in your life... What? You thought that I was joking about making your dream a reality?!

Whilst you're doing that, I'll be having conversations with the Institute of Learning & Management about mapping the content of this trilogy to their courses. If you are interested in gaining a recognised qualification, keep an eye on the website, www.instantimpact.org, where we'll update you on these discussions. My aim is for your work to be assessed, verified, and accredited so you can receive an ILM qualification.

You are not alone. I can also support you with audio books, on social media, podcasts, videos, apps, newsletters, video calls, one-to-one mentoring with me or a trusted member of my team, online courses, and small group training where we can work through the activities in this trilogy together in person. If we can help you in any way, please email: hello@instantimpact.org

Look! The sun is finally burning away those dark clouds Sunflower, lift your head and sparkle, be glorious!

Phase _____	Milestone Planner	
Month	Task	Lead

Appendices

Photo: Bessi Hamiti, Pixabay

"Dwell on the beauty of life. Watch the stars and see yourself running with them."
Marcus Aurelius

"I wasn't a financial pro, and I paid the price"
Ruth Handler

Jelly baby colours

Each of us has a favourite colour that reflects something about our personalities. The following interpretations give a general indication. Intense shades of a colour often indicate extreme traits. These are listed under each colour interpretation.

Red

Attributes: A high-energy person, someone with unlimited resources who is always on the move.
Intensified attributes: A highly-strung, highly emotional person who is prone to excessive stress.

Orange

Attributes: a balanced personality, someone who weighs logic with emotion, a positive thinker.
Intensified attributes: An imbalance in the personality.

Yellow

Attributes: The intellectual, logic is all-important, everything must be orderly. A sunny personality but is often picky.
Intensified attributes: Logical to the point of being rigid.

Green

Attributes: A changeable personality. A person who is always looking ahead, wanting to grow.
Intensified attributes: An emotional chameleon, flighty and fickle, envious, sometimes deceitful, and duplicitous.

Blue

Attributes: A private person, a loner a solitary personality who looks within. The peacekeeper.
Intensified attributes: A lonely, depressed person who keeps everything inside.

Purple

Attributes: A person with an established way of thinking who is bound by numerous rules and regulations. Habits from the past or religion may provide the guidelines this person seeks.
Intensified attributes: Someone with many self-imposed restrictions and limitations. A rigid and unyielding personality.

Brown

Attributes: Security conscious, earthy, with both feet on the ground, a stable person.
Intensified attributes: Self-centred, insecure, and materialistic.

Guess what my favourite colour is?!?

Pink

Attributes: eternal romantic, loving life, health conscious.
Intensified attributes: Concerned about love, health, and vitality but from a pessimistic point of view.

Peach

Attributes: Someone who is romantic but balanced. A warm, mellow personality who is upbeat.
Intensified attributes: No intensive attributes for peach.

Violet

Attributes: A spiritually orientated person who is concerned with the higher order of things. This person has little interest in mechanical, mundane activities.
Intensified attributes: No intensive attributes for violet.

Gold

Attributes: this is the colour of the high-achiever, a goal-setting person who is usually successful in all they undertake.
Intensified attributes: No intensive attributes for gold.

Silver

Attributes: An intuitive personality, this individual must be careful not to build "castles in the air".
Intensified attributes: No intensive attributes for silver.

Grey

Attributes: Confusion reigns, the true personality is bogged down by muddled thoughts.
Intensified attributes: No intensive attributes for grey.

Black

Attributes: A hidden personality, someone with secrets.
Intensified attributes: No intensive attributes for black.

White

Attributes: An understanding person who looks deeply into all sides of an issue yet remains uninvolved.
Intensified attributes: No intensive attributes for white.

Rainbow (mixed colours)

Attributes: A person who fluctuates from being a positive thinker to a negative one but is nevertheless lucky. This person can adjust to almost any circumstance.
Intensified attributes: No intensive attributes for rainbow.

The Rainbow Oracle, Tony Grosso & Rob MacGregor, Ballantine Books, 1989

Personal financial statement

Name

Address

Owned/rented

Telephone

Dependents

Income	Monthly £	Priority debts	Monthly £
Income (take home)	£	Rent/mortgage arrears	£
Rent	£	Council Tax arrears	£
Other	£	Heating arrears	£
Other	£	Lighting arrears	£
Other	£	Water arrears	£
Other	£	Telecoms arrears	£
Other	£	Insurance premium	£
Total income	**£**	**Total priority debts**	**£**

Expenditure	Monthly £	Income minus debts	Monthly £
Rent	£	Money left (after expenditure)	£
Mortgage	£	**Minus**	
Council Tax	£	Total priority payments	£
House insurance	£	**Money left for creditors**	£
Car insurance	£		
Pet insurance	£	**Non-priority debts**	**Monthly £**
Heating	£	Debt 1	£
Lighting	£	Debt 2	£
Water	£	Debt 3	£
Telecoms, phone, internet	£	Other	£
Mobile phone	£	Other	£
TV licence	£	Other	£
Transport/fuel	£	Other	£
Food and sundries	£	Other	£
Clothes	£	Other	£
Prescriptions	£	Other	£
Mobile phone insurance	£	Other	£
Total expenditure	**£**	**Total repayments**	**£**
Total income	£	Money left for creditors	£
Minus		**Minus**	
Total expenditure	£	Total repayments	£
Money left	**£**	**Money left**	**£**

I declare that the above information concerning my financial circumstances is correct.

I offer to pay £ _____ **a month.** Signed _____ Date _____

Planning for Fabulous

January	July

February	August

March	September

April	October

May	November

June	December

My Treasure Map

Your secret jotter

"He who knows all the answers has not been asked all the questions."
Confucius

If you need more space for any of the activities in this book, please use these pages.

You can also use these pages to work up your answers in rough before copying them neatly into the main. book.

Alternatively, email hello@instantimpact.org with "Invisible Playbook" in the subject line. I'll send you a document that expands as you type.

Your secret jotter

"We have two lives, and the second begins when we realise we only have one."

Confucius

Your secret jotter

"Respect yourself and others will respect you."
Confucius

Photo: Alexas Fotos, Pixabay

Your secret jotter

"Roads were made for journeys, not destinations."
Confucius

Photo: Alexas Fotos, Pixabay

Your secret jotter

"I hear and I forget.
I see and I remember.
I do and I understand."
Confucius

Your secret jotter

"The journey of 1,000 miles begins with one step."
Confucius

Photo: Meriç Tuna, Unsplash

"Life is really simple, but we insist on making it complicated."
Confucius

Ingram Content Group UK Ltd.
Milton Keynes UK
UKHW050631180623
423630UK00005B/14